Hotelier
Thoughts

Leadership Traits
Operational Priorities

ISBN: 979-8-218-33120-7

Introduction

For many years I had the idea to write a book that would help and inspire others. For so long I wanted to start but something kept holding me, I was still thinking about the core idea of the book and finally it was the right moment. Success is a journey not a destination like they say and now, after years of experience, the message I want to deliver is clear.

Which leadership traits are most important if you want to succeed and rise to the top?

What operational priorities must you concentrate on if you want to operate a successful hotel business?

I am like you, always looking for answers and guidance. You are probably reading this book as you are looking to gain more knowledge and further your career.

Are you trying to find the right path? You probably want to know a little about me before going through this book. I have had a great career in hotel management over the years.

I am originally from Egypt and acquired American citizenship at a later stage in life after working for many years in the USA. My family did not spare any efforts in my education, and they are the ones responsible for who I have become today.

Once I obtained my bachelor's degree in hotel management, I set my mind on higher education and attained my master's degree from one of the best universities in our field, Florida International University (F.I.U.), Miami, Florida, where I graduated with a Master of Science degree in hotel and food service management.

Throughout my career, I had the honor to work for some prestigious hotel companies across the globe, such as Marriott, Movenpick, Melia, Shaza, and Steigenberger hotels and resorts by Deutsche Hospitality, in addition to a couple of independently owned large properties. My thirty-five years' experience spans from the USA to North Africa, the Middle East, and GCC countries.

I have worked in almost every hotel type (resort, city, airport, convention, extended-stay lodging, etc.).

I have managed many hotels and completed many successful hotel openings and conversions.

This experience made me who I am today, and I am very proud of my career. I held many positions over the years, starting as a front desk clerk and reaching the position of Area Director of Operations for two countries.

The most important part of my career is that "I Love What I Do," and in the pages to come, I will share with you some of my philosophies and thoughts on what I believe is the road to success. I was influenced by many great leaders throughout my career who guided my thoughts and helped me succeed.

In the pages to come, I am highlighting key leadership traits and important operational priorities that will not only help guide your thoughts but also be inspirational and educational. I am confident you will enjoy reading this book and take something from it. I hope you will find your path and be inspired to be your best and be successful.

Table of Contents

Formula for Success

Self - Awareness

Formula for Success

Success is not always simple; it requires a combination of performance, attitude, and knowledge. However, the degree to which you apply each of these components and how other people view you are the two most crucial components for success.

So, do you really know your capabilities? Do you really know your strengths and weaknesses? It's time for an in-depth self-assessment. Self-awareness is critical to your success. Those who know where they stand are the ones who take calculated decisions to impact their future and be more successful.

"Your past impacts your present, which you cannot change,
but the present is in your hands,
and whatever you do will impact your future."

Let's look at those factors to see how they can influence your future.

Knowledge

Success depends on it, and it has an immediate effect on your "performance."

Depending on background education, experience, and exposure over time, each person's level of knowledge varies.

As you worked at different jobs over the years to get to where you are now, you accumulated experience. Will this do? Most likely not, since we constantly seek to learn new things as time goes on, and you ought to be aware of your position.

As a result, the extent of your knowledge is determined by the range of factors that are specific to the job or jobs you have held. Before beginning any task, you must be confident in your own abilities and fully aware of the scope of your knowledge.

Knowledge Capabilities

They are defined by your strengths and weaknesses, so in order to define both, you will need to measure and self-assess your knowledge in relation to your job role.

This is a common question you are usually asked during a job interview. Many managers stumble on this question and think twice before answering, but successful leaders know exactly where they stand.

You must complete a self-assessment of your knowledge and capabilities and be honest with yourself. Assess your knowledge first based on your current role, then do the exercise again considering future or desired roles.

The main factors include:

- Professional know-how
- Technical skills
- Financial skills

The assessment's section on interpersonal and communication skills will be completed later.

In order to determine your abilities and strengths, you must analyze each of the aforementioned factors in great detail. The areas where you excel and feel at ease performing are usually your areas of strength. You must pay close attention to your areas of weakness and develop a strategy to overcome them.

"Your confidence, self-esteem, and performance
are driven largely by your knowledge."

There are many ways to strengthen your area of weakness, but the most crucial thing is that you have the motivation to do so in order to grow as a leader. Over the years, I have encountered numerous managers who don't confront their fears, underperform, or run away from the challenge. We constantly learn new things throughout our lives, so don't be that manager.

Depending on your managerial position, the depth of knowledge needed varies by level, but all managers must have basic knowledge of common elements. A general manager might not have extensive experience in one or more of the departments but will need knowledge of basic elements in order to manage the performance of such departments and be able to increase productivity and maximize returns.

"Knowledge is power."

I have discovered that this is incredibly true over the years. It is the engine that propels our high-speed performance. It serves as the foundation for your capacity for decision-making. You must increase your knowledge across the board, especially in your areas of weakness, to become a well-rounded manager.

In this fast-moving world, things evolve rapidly around us every day with new methods and new ways. Your knowledge will not be complete without keeping up with these new trends. You have to be well connected to new facets of your industry through various channels, including social media, which has helped us connect with the world and see things faster.

"It is those leaders who identify new ideas and implement them, that make the elite team of top performers."

So now take a deep breath and start planning to improve your areas of need through training, cross-exposure, or even education.

Performance

It is another key element of success. Once backed with solid knowledge, performance is the engine of delivery. It is measured by the things you do and the decisions you make day after day to reach your goals. It is also measured by the end results of your decisions, which can be financial or non-financial.

So, all the tasks and interactions you have to perform on a daily, weekly, and monthly basis determine how effective you are? You have to ensure that your hard work is noticed and will achieve the desired results. Consequently, those tasks and interactions are driven by a set of objectives and priorities, which are the main drivers.

Objectives and Priority

To perform well, you need to prioritize your work and have a clear understanding of your objectives. It's easier said than done, but hold on a second; it is actually a very simple process and based on your goals.

"Successful managers start with the end in mind
and know exactly where they want to go."

The characteristics of your objectives and must be "SMART"

- **S**pecific
- **M**easurable
- **A**chievable
- **R**esult oriented
- **T**ime Specific

Once the picture is clear about where you want to go, now comes the issue of "priority" in your day-to-day duties. You need to prioritize your tasks based on their importance and how they fit into achieving your objectives. Some managers do spend a lot of time doing things that are not directly related to achieving those results and hence waste a lot of valuable time.

Every action you take in your day-to-day activities must be related to one of those objectives to drive it forward; otherwise, you will never get to see the desired results or will get there late. In our demanding world, owners have so much investment at stake and want fast, efficient results.

"If you don't act fast, you will be left behind."

You must first clearly understand the priorities of both your management company and the owning company. Those priorities take the highest attention in your day-to-day tasks, followed by your other priorities. Your daily tasks must be categorized into one of the below quadrants to help you make better use of your time. Each quadrant has its own style of leadership to get the job done efficiently.

Tasks	Urgent	Not Urgent
Important	Do	Plan
Not Important	Delegate	Eliminate

- Important and urgent tasks take the highest priority on your list, which you have to "do" yourself and complete in a timely fashion to meet the due dates.

- Important but not urgent tasks come next on your priority list, and those you can "plan" ahead to complete when you have more time.

- Not important but urgent tasks you must "delegate" to someone else to follow. Do not waste your time on these, and make sure you allocate them to the right person.

- Not important and not urgent tasks you must "Eliminate". They are a waste of your time and efforts and have no impact on your goals.

If you consistently follow the above chart, you will have organized your priorities well and know how to best spend your time to be more effective.

Each day, you should make sure you plan and prepare a quick list of the important tasks you need to complete for the following day, review the next day's schedule of meetings, and make sure you plan free time to handle any unexpected tasks that pop up during the day. Every task scheduled should relate to one of the objectives you target based on its importance level.

All your scheduled tasks should fall into the important quadrants; otherwise, make sure you delegate or eliminate.

"Performance relates to doing the things that matter in a timely fashion, according to their priority levels, to achieve results."

Your performance is also determined by the effectiveness of your order-giving and decision-making capabilities. So, if you know your objectives and priorities well but don't use proper techniques to deliver them, you will not achieve your goals. Delegating tasks, holding people accountable, and eventually following up are key factors in ensuring the plan works.

Similar to knowledge capabilities, now you must complete a self-assessment of your performance capabilities and be honest with yourself. Assess your performance first based on your current role, then do the exercise again considering future or desired roles.

The main factors include:

- People engagement skills
- Planning skills
- Time management skills
- Communication skills
- Decision-making skills

Attitude

Last but not least, "attitude," which represents fifty percent of the formula for success. I have always believed that no matter how good your knowledge and performance capabilities are, you will never achieve success without a positive attitude.

The famous quote stayed with me for years..

"Your attitude determines your altitude."

It is the driver through which you use your "knowledge" to consistently and efficiently deliver "performance" and ultimately achieve success.

Why is attitude so important?

It drives your behavior, which impacts everyone and everything around you. More importantly, it impacts you and your self-esteem.

Over the years, people have developed many theories on how to control their attitude and be more positive.

It is proven that looking at things in a positive manner promotes conscious behavior, which allows you to get things done more efficiently and faster.

Every action you take will have a reaction, and in simple words, every positive action will have a positive reaction, and vice versa, a negative attitude will only generate a negative reaction.

To control your attitude, you must learn to harness the power of your brain. Every day, you have the choice of whether to have a positive or negative attitude.

Remember that effective leaders are those who have the ability to control their attitude and, in turn, their behavior.

Some days, other external factors will have an impact on how you feel and behave. When interacting with guests, hospitality professionals are constantly reminded to smile and put their problems aside. The same is true for actors; once they step onto the stage, they put their problems aside and live the life of their characters. You as a manager or a leader in your company are not exempt from this. Put all your problems behind you before you go on to the stage and be positive.

Leaders impact and drive the attitude of their teams, and they must lead by example. You must truly believe that your behavior reflects on your team, positively or negatively. It is in your hands to set the attitude and tone of your team to establish the most productive environment to get things done effectively and in a timely fashion.

"Success does not come easy,

it is a combination of hard work (Performance),

continuous learning (Knowledge)

and a positive mind (Attitude).

Don't Miss the Train

Planning & Proactivity

Don't miss the train

We have all heard the term "failing to plan is planning to fail." Think about it for a second: in this fast-paced, evolving world, planning is key to success. Without a plan in place, you stand no chance of succeeding; it is as simple as this.

So, do you have a plan? Are you proactive? or you just go with the flow. If your answer is "no," then you have missed the train and will not make it to your destination on time.

But wait! Can you start now and catch up? The answer is "Yes, you can."

They say "you don't get a second chance to make a first impression, but I am a firm believer that you can get a second chance to positively change that first impression and create a new one." Whether you are planning for the first impression or attempting to change it, don't miss the train. You need the perfect "plan," and you need to be "proactive" to save and direct this plan.

Planning

It refers to the process of setting goals, developing

strategies, and outlining tasks and schedules to accomplish the goals. It also helps in defining objectives both in quantitative and qualitative terms.

"Planning is a fundamental element to reaching your goals on time, which is your road map to success."

A key element of the plan is that it is written and documented so it can be looked at and followed. This is your road map and guide to what you want to achieve. But if the plan is written but stored and forgotten, what use will it be? If you don't look at your map as a guide, you will lose your way.

"If it is written, it shall be done."

In the management world, planning is vital as it helps to clarify, focus, and track the project's development and prospects. It also provides a logical framework within which a business can develop and pursue business strategies in the future. It also provides a benchmark against which actual performance can be measured and reviewed.

The Plan

Preparing a solid plan requires some work, so let us review the key elements needed to develop your plan:

- Identify the purpose of your work plan.
- Write the introduction and background.
- List your goals and objectives (SMART).
- List your resources.
- Identify any constraints.
- Identify who is accountable.
- List action steps to reach each goal or objective.
- Write down your overall strategy.

Once you have completed your plan, make sure it is shared with all team members for feedback to ensure they will buy into it, and then request that they break down all the objectives with more specific tasks into their own plan in the same way. This is your road map and the measurement tool, which should be updated regularly with the team.

You see, the planned activities, or "tasks" will break down every step of what needs to be done and the required resources. It is what you depend on during the journey.

"If the plan does not work, change the plan,

but never the goal."

Proactivity

It is your means to anticipate things that can go wrong, take corrective action, and re-direct your course. Many external factors affect our plans, and it is in our best interest to stay focused on our targets. As we know, different inputs can result in different outputs.

Which one do you prefer? to take things into your hands by being "proactive"? or let things surprise you and be out of your control by being "reactive"?

I can hear your answer that you want to stay ahead of the game, but how? It can all be under your control with a simple notion.

"Proactive thinking includes

anticipating all the obstacles before they come

and exploring all the possibilities to overcome them."

Easier said than done? may be, but it is a matter of habit. Proactive managers were not born proactive, but they trained themselves to do so. To anticipate things before they happen and to always explore "what if" situations.

It is a state of mind that you must always place yourself in as a successful leader. The higher you move up the ladder, the more this is expected of you.

"You think for others, and you think ahead."

When you do so, you will see various and new possibilities that you never thought of before; you will see things that might happen before they do; and you will be able to change course before it affects your plan. You are in full control.

"Failing to plan is planning to fail."

Winners and Losers

Negotiations and Decisions

Winners and Losers

During the years, I have been inspired by many writers, especially Steven Covey, who wrote the amazing book "Seven Habits of Highly Effective People." Mr. Covey's approach to leadership is that it all relates to your habits, day in and day out.

Since the start of my career, I have worked as a front office manager at a luxury five-star hotel in Washington, D.C., USA, under the leadership of a great general manager who spent a lot of time and effort building and developing the team to drive performance.

He believed deeply in Mr. Covey's philosophy and invited the entire management team to a remote location, where he spent several days teaching us these habits. He wanted to make sure the message was clear and that we bought into this philosophy. I found out that successful leaders have certain good habits that they live with every moment of their lives.

One of the habits that I admire is called "win-win," which deals with negotiations and decision-making process.

Once back from the trip, we spent a full year just practicing what we had learned until it became a "habit."

He has changed my life since that moment with such great leadership, which has widened my understanding of the world we live in and made me more successful. If you want to achieve success, you have to build good habits in both your personal and professional lives.

Win-Win

The "win-win" habit turned out to be one of the most useful leadership traits that I have followed throughout my career. It is simply based on the notion that we all win together to achieve sustained short- and long-term gains. Everyone in your circle must have some success for life to go on. You cannot be the only winner all the time. It is just common sense, which helps you in every decision you make.

Having said this, it does not mean there are no losers or that you might lose sometimes. But think about it in every decision you have to make. *Does my win break the other person emotionally or financially?*

Is he going to perform well again?

Will he stand by me the next time I need him?

In the hotel business, we are faced with many daily decisions, and every time I decide on an issue, I wonder if I am fair in my decision? What impact will this decision have on the other person? I realized quickly that it is imperative that we all win in order to keep the business successful. We have to reach a "compromise" in what we do in many situations otherwise, we reach a dead end and in many cases we lose.

"Win-win" requires consideration and courage;
reaching a compromise is the best scenario to sustain gains."

As an example, if your hotel is located in a remote destination and a vendor has rented one of your shops for a fixed monthly rent, his business is based on the hotel's occupancy and the number of guests you have in house. His contract clearly states that he pays a specific amount per month.

Now that your business has dropped for a couple of months, the outlook for the next few months is bleak, and the vendor approaches you and requests a reduction in the monthly rent; otherwise, he will be out of business.

The services offered by this shop are critical to your customer satisfaction, and now you are faced with a decision. Should you hold the vendor accountable for the monthly rent as per the contract, or should you reach a compromise on the rent amount to ensure he will continue to offer the service to your guests?

Of course, the answer to this question would have some implications on your revenues, but you're faced with a choice to either accept receiving reduced amounts and keep the revenue stream along with the services offered to your guests, or to insist on enforcing a contract condition, which eventually would drive them out of business and ultimately you would lose both the revenue and guest satisfaction. Obviously, in this situation, you have to reach a compromise where both parties are winners. This is what we call "win-win."

The decisions you make can actually make you win in the short term, but in the long term you could lose, so every time you make a decision, you have to consider these factors and the implications of your decision to remain a winner in the future.

"Remember, what goes around comes around."

The "win-win" concept is used in every facet of our lives, not only in the workplace, but you should apply it with your family, friends, and coworkers in order for life to go on. I cannot begin to express how the "win-win" habit has made me successful over the past years in being able to reach a compromise in very difficult negotiation situations and satisfying all parties.

Lose-Win

Sometimes you have to lose in order to win in the long term. There are some situations where you actually decide to take the loss and delay the win until another day; this is the toughest part of making a decision. After you study all the facts, you might realize that

"Short-term losses can generate much higher long-term gains."

Let me elaborate with an example: one of your employees has committed an act that is considered gross misconduct, and he is one of your best workers. You are now faced with a very tough decision to uphold your policies and procedures and the labor law by terminating him.

So, what would you do?

In this situation, unfortunately, you have to take the loss in order to make long-term gains. You can't compromise your policies and those of the law; otherwise, you are opening the door for others to act the same, and you will be expected to treat them equally.

"Lose-Win requires very high consideration, and short-term loss could generate long-term gains."

In the decision-making process, you have to be fair and consistent and always consider the short-term and long-term implications.

You have a sensible choice to make based on the situation. In this case, making the hard decisions shows the real character of a leader and will surely have long-term gains. This is what we call "Lose-Win."

Win-Lose

In some circumstances, you might be forced to win while others lose. If you do this, be aware that long-term gains might become difficult, especially if you have to deal with the same person or company that lost.

You see, it is in our nature to want to always win, but take a moment and put yourself in the other person's shoes.

When you lose, you will make every effort in the future to turn the loss into a victory, usually at the expense of the person who beat you last time. So, when you decide to be the only winner, you have to be aware of the consequences. This is what we call "Win-Lose."

"Win-lose has the lowest consideration and will not sustain long-term gains."

Lose-Lose

The worst-case scenario and the least smart one is when no one is a winner and both parties lose. When this happens, it means we failed to reach a compromise, we failed to understand that short-term losses can lead to long-term gains, and we failed to communicate properly and explore all possibilities.

It means our ego has taken over and blinded our decision. You don't want to be in this situation ever again, as you might not recover from such a loss and will not find the support in the other party to help you rise again.

It is inevitable that this could happen sometimes, depending on the circumstances. This is what we call "Lose-Lose".

"Lose-Lose requires low consideration and low courage;
it's not a smart move."

So next time you are faced with a choice, make your decision wisely based on the above notions and always consider the short- and long-term implications.

"Win - Win"

Requires consideration and courage.

Reaching a compromise is the best scenario to sustain gains.

"Win - Lose"

Has the lowest consideration.

Will not sustain long-term gains.

"Lose - Win"

Requires very high consideration.

Short-term losses could generate long-term gains.

"Lose - Lose"

Requires low consideration and low courage.

Not a smart move.

The Ultimate Balance

Building Trust

The Ultimate Balance

A crucial subject that general managers don't often discuss enough is how to strike a balance between the company's interests and priorities and that of the owners. This is a challenge that inexperienced managers deal with on a daily basis; in certain cases, it can damage their reputation and even result in their termination. It can be challenging to find the balance between the two, and it calls for persistence, understanding, and effective communication.

Your profound comprehension of the extent and character of the partnership between the managing company and the owning company will help you to answer this question. To ascertain the essential "priorities" for each party as well as the degree of "trust" between them, you must pay close attention to what is being said and observed.

To take a preference for one side over the other will put you in a difficult situation and cause conflict. Your goal is to establish a "win-win" scenario where both parties.

Comprehending the management agreement in its entirety is imperative as it establishes legal obligations for both sides and elucidates their respective responsibilities. The terms of the agreement shall serve as the foundation for all of your decisions. You will be heard and respected by all parties if you act in this manner on a regular basis. Take care not to go overboard; owners may find it annoying when managers frequently say things like "as per the management agreement." Occasionally, rather than the legal details of the relationship, all they want to hear is sound logic and an explanation of the circumstances.

It is important that you share the owner's perspective with your boss and keep them informed about all relevant issues.

"Building trust in both directions

is crucial to your success."

The majority of management agreements contain a provision enabling the owners to choose who gets hired and replaced in executive roles, particularly those of "financial controller" and "general manager."

This is standard procedure in the sector because these two do have significant influence over financial transactions and decision-making. Mistrust will eventually grow between the owners and the manager if they believe the ship is not sailing in the right direction or if they believe the managers are more devoted to their company. Many managers fall into this trap, and you don't want to be one of them.

It is imperative to consider both the nature of the organization and the kind of owner or owner representative you are collaborating with. Some owners are merely investors and have little understanding of the business of running a hotel. As a result, they frequently make poor decisions that damage the company's operations and strain their relationship with the management company. It will take a lot of work on your part to constantly justify what you are doing to those kinds of owners.

"You always have to show the end result and the return on investment."

It's important to keep in mind that these owners primarily consider financial gains; if you can consistently demonstrate to them the potential benefits of your actions, you will win a lot of battles. If your outcomes are as expected, you will gradually gain the owner's trust until you are in a safe place.

Other owners who understand the business and have been involved in similar projects will actually be easier to deal with, as they will understand your reasoning on many occasions, but unfortunately, they will also have more tough goals to reach and will tend to interfere in the decision-making process to achieve their goals. Smart managers use this to their advantage and try to level with those owners as their partners in the business and really appreciate their input, which must be discussed. Be careful not to become a "yes sir," and if the owner's direction does not meet your targets, you should overcome this tactfully.

"You must professionally negotiate and
redirect the discussion in an
objective and convincing manner."

Never undervalue the knowledge of the owner. The majority of owners value a manager who is straightforward, truthful, knows the subject, asks for their understanding, and values their input in general. You may be familiar with the phrase "managing the owner," which has gained importance in today's business world and is essential to general managers' success in relieving pressure.

"Managing the owner means

keeping lines of communication open at all times;

the owner is approachable, and so are you."

The owner feels comfortable approaching you with his worries so that you two can work out a solution. A warning sign should be raised if the owner begins to go around you and deal directly with your boss. This indicates that you have not been managing him properly.

Some other owners may be involved in your business on multiple levels as they operate through organizations and have multiple tiers within the company. It's ideal for general managers to centralize communication and decision-making, but if this isn't possible, you'll need to modify your management approach to deal with disruptions and ensure that you're informed. In the event that such a scenario arises, you ought to collaborate closely with your group to ensure that you are fully apprised of any correspondence with the owner's business.

Any decision that your team needs to make can only be made with the General Manager's guidance and approval, "preferably through the GM office." If this isn't feasible, the responsible Manager has to make it clear in his correspondence that the GM has reviewed and approved the matter in question. It's not intentional for these organizations to avoid you; it's just the way they work. If you participate in all decision-making processes, you will begin to earn their respect and trust.

Managing Relationship

Below are some important key points to manage your relationship in both directions and keep it healthy:

- Keep both parties well informed.
- Be honest in all your encounters and always use facts.
- Communicate with owners and your boss on regular

basis

- Be on time and never miss a deadline.

- Owner requests are top priority, so deal with them swiftly.

- Be proactive and anticipate what they are looking for at all times.

- Know which battles to fight; "don't win the war and lose the battle."

- Know the owner's priorities in relation to the operation and make sure it happens.

- Always show your plans to control costs; it's mostly about money.

"The ultimate balance is to be fair and honest, manage priorities, and always seek a win-win solution."

As a leader or department head, building trust with your team and your immediate manager is also key to your success. You also have to align your priorities with those of the company and those of your manager. All the above-mentioned points about managing the relationship hold very true for you and your boss, as you want to earn the trust and respect.

You need your immediate manager to believe in you and your capabilities. You need him to guide you to learn more, be successful, and progress your career. You need him to appreciate your work and give you fair evaluation on your annual review. You need him to recommend you for the next steps.

You see, building trust with your manager is crucial to your success and career progression. It only comes with hard work, honesty, and building trust.

"Without trust, you will not achieve your goals."

Inspire Me, Inspire You

Motivation

Inspire me, Inspire You

In this chapter, I highlight the issue of "motivation" and its importance to productivity and customer satisfaction. As a leader, this task falls on your shoulders to first motivate yourself and then to motivate your team. It is you who should lead by example to set the stage for those reporting to you.

Is your team inspired and motivated to do their job?

Are they happy and productive?

There are many questions to answer, but it all starts with you, "The Leader." You are the key person who is responsible for an employee's performance and you have the keys to their motivation and inspiration.

Are you personally inspired and motivated?

If the answer to this question is "yes," then it makes it much easier for you to motivate and inspire others. If the answer is "no," then you need to start with yourself. If your confidence and self-esteem are low, it is difficult, but not impossible, to motivate and inspire others.

"People cannot give what they lack."

You see, the leader's state of mind always impacts those around him. Your mood, your energy level, and your perception are directly transferred to your teams and impact how they feel and perform. You can do your best to hide your feelings and emotions, but people close to you will not be fooled. They will sense what you are going through and be impacted by it.

First, you need to find out the real reasons for your lack of motivation. This can only be done by being honest with yourself, finding the root cause, and tackling it. Whether it is a personal issue or a work-related issue, there is something you can do to change it.

They say "you should leave your personal life outside the door when you arrive to work." Yes, you should, and while it is sometimes very difficult to do so, you should force your full concentration at work and don't let those issues impact your performance or, more importantly, your attitude.

You should make every attempt to fix those personal issues to live a happy life and reduce your stress.

If your lack of motivation is work-related, you have to identify the core problem and tackle it head-on. Whether it is your employer or your owner, you must immediately have a direct dialogue to clarify and solve these issues. Don't hesitate; every problem has a solution. Call your boss and discuss your dissatisfaction at once. Be clear and honest and in most cases, you will reach an understanding that will relieve your concerns. Happy, inspired, and motivated managers are able to inspire others to get the job done, to meet their targets, and to appreciate what they do, even if it requires very hard work. The employees get their energy from you.

Inspirational Leaders

- Smile and be well groomed.
- Have self-confidence.
- Communicate clearly and meet regularly.
- Ensure the team is well informed.
- Lead by example in all aspects.
- Have an open-door policy and listen carefully to employees' feedback.

- Be fair and consistent with their decisions.

- Reach out to all, don't leave someone behind.

- Show concern for people's well-being and feelings.

- Respect yourself and respect others.

- Be creative and encourage new ideas.

- Be courageous, and don't be afraid to fail.

- Coaching and counseling should be done in private, not in public.

- Reward and recognize achievements through various means.

You should know that a simple "thank you" goes a very long way and motivates people more than you can imagine, especially when done in front of others. Make sure your "People Engagement" department has implemented all sorts of recognition and well-being programs.

Employees Well-Being

- They live well and rest well in their accommodations "If staff housing is offered".

- They eat well and are healthy.

- They are compensated well, according to a market

competitive survey.

- They are incentivized when they meet their targets.

- They have enough activities outside of the workplace to encourage teamwork.

- They have a well-designed and comfortable uniform. This will add to their self-confidence and pride in the workplace.

- They have the proper tools and supplies to do the job.

Having said this, the most important motivational factor for employees, aside from "money and recognition," is their own "training and development" for career progression. You must always consider development plans and succession planning for your employees to make sure they are motivated and that the right caliber is ready for promotion to the next level.

"An inspirational leader is always in the front,
always caring for others."

Show Case

Presentations

Show Case

One of the key elements of success is to properly present yourself and your work in a professional and timely manner. Communication is vital to linking you and your organization to the world around you. You have to spend lots of time and energy focused on this; otherwise, all that you do can go unrecognized, and you would not be effective or perceived well. You have to showcase yourself and portray the right image.

"Showcase" is an art that can be taught and applied. It is a mix of various communication methods and means that will project your performance and results to the world around you. The who, when, and how are totally in your hands.

How can you go about it?

What is it exactly you want to show, and by what means?

Note that too little and too much can be wrongly perceived, and you might not get the desired results. You need to find the perfect balance in order to be effective, and keep that in mind.

"Perception is reality."

So, on a daily basis, you have different groups with whom you have to communicate for various reasons. First, you need to identify the groups, then the purpose. Each one has its own priorities and requirements, and you need to communicate equally in all directions to be effective.

Those groups can be:

- Owner

- Superiors

- Co-workers and employees

- Guests

You will need to allocate time to communicate with each, depending on your priorities.

"Your communication through various channels must be consistent, regular, and fact-based."

In this section, I want to focus on how you show yourself to the world so you can get the most returns. Before going through the characteristics of communication, there are some fundamental elements that you need to make sure are in place.

Personal Appearance

Your professional attire and hygiene are of the utmost priority, and they send subliminal messages about who you are. Don't let your guard down at any time, and stick to the professional outfit when in touch with any of the groups. Sharp-looking, well-dressed managers are perceived differently than others and give a sense of confidence.

Attitude

As expressed earlier, your positive attitude plays a big part in your success. Being open-minded, compassionate, and welcoming are characteristics of a successful leader that go a very long way and will allow your thoughts to be heard. Don't underestimate this; people often turn away from snobbish managers with high egos who think they know it all. You want to be portrayed as approachable and understanding, and people should feel at ease talking to you.

Organization

People respect those who are well organized. This starts in

your office, where it is neat, tidy, and well organized.

Empty or clean desks do not mean you are not working; they mean you got the job done and are ready for the next job. Make sure you have a proper filing system, hard copy or soft copy, that you can easily access to find the information you need.

This is a super powerful part of showcasing yourself. When approached by anyone, you should be readily able to reach this information instantly and start the discussion.

Verbal and written communication

- Verbal communication must be professional at all times, using the appropriate address for people.
- Don't miss due dates; always be on time. If you can't make the due date, ask for an extension and give reasons.
- Always present your communication in a professional manner, well written, spell-checked, and based on facts.
- Use proper addressing to the people you communicate with and think twice about who is

supposed to be copied on your correspondence as copying everyone is not a good practice.

- Be objective in your message, listing facts, findings, and finally a conclusion and recommendations.

- Get all the facts so the message can be conclusive before replying, and don't wait for someone to tell you they need more information.

- Always portray a positive message and leave the door open for more discussion.

- Don't blame others when things go wrong; simply list the facts.

- Bring new initiatives to the table; don't just follow up on existing ones. You can think, you are creative, and you have ideas, so why not share them?

- Support your company's priorities and seek a win-win situation.

Reports and Presentations

Your communication can sometimes be associated with reports and presentations. Depending on your level of experience in preparing such reports, you must always deliver a top-notch presentation using the proper templates and sequence of events.

Many managers send reports that look sloppy and incomplete, using the wrong formats and fonts. This is very irritating to others and sends the wrong message.

The characteristics of the reports and presentations are:

- accurate, precise, and factual.
- colorful with proper highlights.
- Using company templates.
- built to attract attention in logical order with purpose, facts, and recommendations.

You see, the impression and perception you portray to the world are based on your physical appearance and communication skills through verbal, written, and presentation means. This, along with facts, objectivity, and a positive attitude, will give others the professional look you desire.

When you have a scheduled meeting always be well prepared and on time. Sit with confidence with straight posture, listen carefully and share your thoughts.

Respect other's opinion even if it differs from yours and speak with facts not emotions.

Having said this, the personal touch is also critical. Whether it is business or social, you must always show the caring and human factor to connect with others. Caring is what makes you bond with people and makes you get their full attention and, in many cases, their support and understanding. Arrogant managers often get resistance to their ideas because of the way they act. Yes, show that you know, but don't show that you are the only one who knows, so listen to others and appreciate their opinion even if you don't agree.

"The way you look and act is the way you are perceived."

The Team and Me

Management Style

The Team and Me

It is not an easy task to build the perfect team and achieve cohesiveness in the workplace. As a matter of fact, it is an art, and you have been trained and coached all your career for this moment. It is your turn to build the perfect team that you trust and that will help you win and achieve the desired goals.

As in sports, the perfect team is the one that has the most members who complement each other and do their part well for the team to succeed. Any weak player will impact performance, and you will find yourself constantly looking for ways to cover his shortfalls and asking others to fill in his shoes. If everyone is well trained, well positioned, motivated, and knows their part of the plan and what is expected of them, then you will have a very high chance of success.

Building your team at work is exactly the same. You will be faced with many challenges as you assemble the perfect team to reach your goals. Let us break down this important notion into several steps.

Once your team is selected, you should ensure everyone is working under one vision, one mission, and a common goal. Each member must know his job role and what is expected of him very clearly, and he must also have his own individual goals that complement the overall targets.

It is important to align the company's strategy with both management and employees' expectations. You will notice that all three meets on a common ground where performance becomes very high.

Each of your team members will have his own personality, strengths, and weaknesses, which you should learn very well in order to manage the team effectively.

You should be able to highlight and focus on the strengths of each member while at the same time depressing their weaknesses or working with them on a development plan.

Once those are identified, it is easier for you to assign the members to the tasks according to their strengths to get the most out of the team.

Management style is a crucial factor in your success. It is how you approach each member based on his characteristics with a different management style in order to get the most out of him.

Each of your employees can be identified into a group based on two major factors;

Commitment

Reflects his or her attitude and willingness to do the job consistently.

Competence

Reflects his or her level of technical skills and knowledge required to do the job.

Employee's Assessment

Once you have completed a quick assessment for each of your team members, they will fall into one of the below quadrants.

Scale	High Commitment	Low Commitment
High Competence	Q1	Q3
Low Competence	Q2	Q4

Obviously, you would hope that all employees fall into quadrant one with the highest commitment and the highest performance, but in reality, it is not possible, and usually you end up with a mixed bag of employees. Each one requires a certain management style to deal with, which you, as a leader, must apply effectively.

High commitment and high competence (Q1)

Those are your super stars—high performers who go above and beyond. They have a great attitude, are motivated, and have excellent technical skills. They require low moral support and low direction. The management style needed with this group is to "delegate" the responsibility to achieve the goal.

High commitment and low competence (Q2)

Those employees have a great attitude and are motivated, but they are not technically strong. They require low moral support but need more direction on how to do things with specific instructions. The amount of direction and teaching depends on their level of technical skills. You will need to closely supervise the achievement of the goal. The management style needed for this group is "direct." This group is great, as they are always willing to take direction and learn new things.

Low commitment and high competence (Q3)

Those employees have a low attitude, are not motivated, but have high technical skills. Due to their low level of motivation in the workplace, you will be required to give high moral support by listening, encouraging, reinforcing, and providing help in the decision-making process. You need to understand the reasons behind their low morale and try to motivate them. The management style needed with this group is to "involve." They will need positive reinforcement as you go along to get the job done.

Low commitment and low competence (Q4)

Those employees with low attitudes, low motivation, and low technical skills—you wish they were not hired in the first place, and hopefully you have a very limited number of those. They require your full moral support and direction. This group will take the most energy from you and your teams.

They require a lot of explaining, teaching, and encouraging while being supervised very closely. The management style needed with this group is to "explain". Unfortunately, you will need to work extra hard on this group to move them to other quadrants, or eventually they will have to be replaced.

As a leader, applying the correct management style will help your team stay on track and achieve the desired results.

Delegates

Delegated the responsibility of achieving the goal.

No moral support is required.

Directs

Give specific instructions on how to achieve the goal.

No moral support is required.

Involves

Encourage, reinforce, and give moral support.

No technical support is required.

Explains

Encourage, reinforce, and give moral support.

Give specific instructions on how to achieve the goal.

Know Your Stuff

Finding Answers

Know your stuff

I stressed earlier that knowledge and performance associated with a great attitude are the bases for success. As a leader, you must always be on top of your game in all areas, be aware, and be well informed at all times. In this section, I want to focus on the technical aspects of the role of the leader and the information that must be readily accessible in order to succeed. There is so much information you need, and having the facts in hand will make the job much easier to handle.

"When approached by your superiors or owners,

you have to know where you stand, display the facts,

and show where you want to go."

You don't have to memorize all the information, as long as you have immediate access to it when needed. Naturally, it is the financial results that occupy the top position on this chart. The material world we live in is mostly about margins and profits for all parties involved. You want to be ready to answer any questions or inquiries. Depending on your job role in the organization, you should have a clear understanding of and immediate access to pertinent information related to your area of responsibility. Your accessibility to information is critical to your continued success.

Running a business nowadays has become more sophisticated and moves at high speed. As a leader, you need to move at the same speed, or you will be left behind. The most important part is not only having the information available but also having a full understanding of it to help you make the right decisions.

Last but not least, leaders must be visible in the operation at all times, especially during peak periods. Those who manage from the floor are more successful than those who manage from the office. You will not see what goes on in the operation unless you see it with your own eyes. No matter the reports you get from your team, they will not have the same assessment as yours. The employees become more confident and more attentive when they see you in the lead. That is who you are "You are a leader" so you must be visible.

Of course, expertise levels differ from one manager to the other, and sometimes we don't comprehend some of the reports or factors involved, so we need to seek answers.

What Is the Answer

Do you know everything? Of course, you don't.

Actually, nobody does. We are not perfect, and we don't know everything. This is a reality, and no matter how good you are, there will be some areas in which you don't have full comprehension or are not your areas of expertise.

When faced with this, what should you do? Let's explore this because knowledge is power, but what if you don't have particular knowledge in certain areas? You don't want to be perceived as someone who doesn't understand.

Over the years, many leaders ran successful businesses that were virtually outside of their background of expertise, so how did they do it? How can a hotelier manage a hospital? As a matter of fact, it is known that some of the best hospital managers are hoteliers, not doctors, so how can this be true?

The answer is simple:

- The proper use of your managerial and leadership skills.

- The proper use of your resources, namely your expert managers.

- Educating yourself on the key margins, factors, and measurements for those areas where you lack expertise so you are able to understand their performance and redirect the course or make new decisions.

As a general manager, you might not be an expert in certain departments, but in fact, you are directing the leader of such departments. This is only possible if you understand the fundamentals and key factors of such a department, which allows you to assess the performance and direct the course.

There is nothing wrong with not knowing particular elements in certain departments. This is why you have experts for each department. Some managers take this personally and try to hide their lack of knowledge, but trust me, it will show and will impact your decisions.

You should have an open mind to educate yourself and ask questions about what you don't understand. Unfortunately, some leaders are shy about doing this and think they will look weak in front of their managers. On the contrary, a great leadership tool is making sure you hire the right expert manager into that position, that you entrust him to run the department, and that you show him that you depend on his expertise. Last but not least, they are the ones that will educate you on all the critical factors that you should look at and guide you on how to analyze the data.

If you've never done this in the past, go ahead and try it. Call any of your directors or managers and tell them that since he is the expert, you need him to show you all the critical elements of running his department. You will be amazed by what you hear and learn. You will receive information that you never thought of.

Depending on your expert managers is a great motivational tool, especially when you show it to them, and your continued education in these areas will help you improve your knowledge as you go along. The next time, you will know what to look for.

This is very true for every manager in the organization. They need to seek continued information and education from the experts in other departments. We complete each other, and as the leader, you have to promote such practices. It will improve the overall understanding of the teams.

I will not highlight here all the detailed factors for each department that you, as a leader, need to look at, but you need to complete this homework asap for those departments where you are lacking knowledge. You may set up a training session with the regional manager responsible for this department if you don't feel comfortable asking your manager. You can read online through many resources about what you should look for.

At the end, what matters is being able to know what to look for and how to analyze such data to make decisions.

Stressful Times

Handling Stress

Stressful Times

We all had it! I can read your mind, and I am sure you are now having a recollection of those tough times. *What is life without pain?* They say "no pain, no gain." How many times have you seen the light at the end of the tunnel and it turned out to be a train coming towards you?

Too many questions come to mind, including why it happened and how I could have avoided it. It is the circle of life, my friends; some do and some don't, but the key is to survive and move on. Along our path, we had those days and those moments that we thought would never end, and usually there is this close friend that keeps you strong and sane and always pushes you by saying, "You can do it."

Did you anticipate those tough times, or did they just hit you? If you saw it coming, then what have you done to avoid it or lessen the impact? And if you did not see it coming, why is that?

> *"It's not the end of the road, unless*
> *you fail to make the turn."*

The answer to this question lies with you. If you had just

spent enough time to think, "Yes, think ahead," you could have been in a different situation. If you had just read the scene correctly, you would have received a different outcome. Nevertheless, it is inevitable, and at some point, in your life you will face "tough and stressful times."

In this chapter, I prefer to focus on the aftermath, or, in other words, how to survive and recover from tough times. If we dwell too much on what we should have done, then we will not move forward. We need to learn from our mistakes to avoid them happening again in the future, but at the moment, we have to face the consequences of the current situation.

It takes three steps to pull yourself through whatever situation you find yourself in:

- Facts finding.
- Change your state of mind.
- Take action.

Facts Finding

It is the most important element in starting the healing process. You want to understand all the circumstances that led to this situation and what decisions you have made that have generated this outcome.

In fact, you also want to know what decisions you did not make.

"Seek first to understand, then be understood."

Go through a full analysis and assessment of the root causes of this stressful situation, whether work-related or personal-life-related, to determine and understand exactly what went wrong. Of course, there are many external factors that could have impacted the situation that were out of your control. Do not jump to conclusions until you have gathered all the facts in detail. If you don't find the root cause, you will not be able to reverse the impact.

State of Mind

Once you have realized the reason(s), now you need to lift your mindset to a positive state and gather your courage to move on to the next stage of correction. In some severe cases, it is difficult, but remember, it is all in your hands by controlling the mental state of the mind.

"It is crucial that you realize and admit the failure."

Once you have accepted the facts surrounding the failure that led to stressful times, you can move on to the next stage of positive mind-setting.

Now focus your mind, lift your self-esteem, and trust in your abilities. There is virtually nothing that cannot be fixed in our business world; it is your approach on how to handle it that makes the difference and could reverse the impact of the situation in your favor.

"Deep inside, you have to believe that you want to do it and that you trust yourself that you can do it."

Without a positive mindset, strong will and determination, you will not be able to move forward.

Take Action

Once you have gathered the facts, accepted them, and set your mind to a positive state, you are ready to move on to the third and final stage, which is brainstorming all of the possible actions that you can take to reverse the situation. The impact could be in various forms, such as reputation, trust, financial loss, perception, physical, etc.

Each one has its own action steps that can be taken

and certain people that can be involved.

Choose the best course of action you want to take to correct the situation and start implementation. Call the person involved to a meeting to discuss the problem.

Be honest, sincere, direct, factual, and show a willingness to change. Recognize the problem, highlight the facts as to why it happened, and even take responsibility for your shortfalls. Show them that despite the downfall, you remain positive and committed to fixing it and moving on. Finally, present your plan in such a convincing way that you can reverse the negative impression or trend, start a new page, and ask for their support.

This is what people around you want to see. They don't want weak managers who dwell on the past. If you come across in the right way, they will let you in and help you through it.

It is very crucial that you "don't make the same mistake twice as this is when you lose credibility, and things get harder to fix.

When you have completed the above steps and

started your new course of action, stress will be minimized to a great extent but will not be alleviated until you have achieved some new successes, at which time you will be proud of your new win and turnaround of the situation.

"You want to minimize the damage

by fixing what you broke,

believing in yourself that you can do it,

and eventually making decisions to reverse the course,

and produce a new outcome."

Exceptional Circumstances

Crisis Management

Exceptional Circumstances

As life goes on, you cannot avoid having emergencies that are unexpected, no matter how much you prepare for them. While I am writing this book, we are in the midst of a global crisis caused by the Corona COVID-19 virus, which has brought the world to almost a complete stop. It has impacted every country, every business, and every person. No one was prepared; no one anticipated, and I don't blame you. Something on this global scale is hard to predict, but it happens, and here we are trying to survive.

They say the true character of people shows in these tough situations, and this is what I believe. It is true leadership that faces the situation, stays calm, and deals with disasters as they come, trying to minimize the damage. They keep everyone working together and minimize the panic. They take bold decisions to protect their assets and their employees.

Crisis Management

During the past few weeks, with the increased

impact of the Corona virus and governmental decisions impacting our business, I have led a great group of managers in a very tough situation. I remained calm and focused throughout. People looked at me to gain confidence and strength to keep moving and keep fighting. We are all in it together; I need them, and they need me.

So as the crisis began, I was always one step ahead for one simple reason: the priorities were clear:

- Minimize financial loss impact on business.
- Protect the asset.
- Protect the employees physically, emotionally, and financially when possible.
- Help the community and stop the spread of viruses.
- Work hand in hand with the owning company and management company to set strategies.
- Survive

I made sure my team was well informed every step of the way. They supported all decisions made on each of the above priorities.

Yes, sometimes you have to make some sacrifices

for the greater good of others. This is inevitable in every crisis. Some employees will lose their jobs if your financial standing cannot support it.

The hotel business has been hit very hard during this crisis, with some hotels closing for several months and suffering massive financial losses. The end is not near as I write this chapter in April 2020. Many hotels took very quick and decisive measures to reduce costs in all controllable areas (energy, service contracts, food costs, etc.) and all possible expenses that could be stopped or eliminated. Your biggest cost in hotels during a crisis is employee payroll and benefits. People are the most expensive element, and the good ones are hard to replace.

It is inevitable to lose some members of your team, but you have to make considerations for their long-term needs. Your high-performance and loyal employees are the ones you want to protect.

The team understood the severity of the situation and the cost impact on the owning company and elected to receive payroll cuts willingly, and some accepted unpaid leave. This went a long way when presented to owners and was very much appreciated. They are doing their best to support us, and we have done our best to survive together till the last moment.

Having said this, the role of the leader under such circumstances is critical to survival and minimizing impact. The leader must be the one who keeps the ship afloat and thinks ahead of all the possibilities.

"What a leader needs during a crisis are behavior and
a mindset that will prevent them from overreacting
and help them look ahead."

Not all crisis situations are this severe, but we should be ready to react quickly in any given situation.

The Leader's Behavior

Recognizing that you are facing a crisis is the first thing you must acknowledge. Don't underestimate the severity of the situation and assume the worst to be prepared. You can then start to mount a response based on the facts you have on hand.

If this crisis is new in nature or an exceptional case, you

cannot follow the emergency plans you have prepared earlier "unless it is a similar case," and you have to adjust to the new situation with creative improvisation. You might be asked to develop new business practices and make adjustments to keep the business going. The most important factor is your behavior throughout the process until you reach clear grounds.

- Don't act alone, and quickly assemble a team of your top managers who will assist you in the fact-finding and decision-making processes.

- Assess as much as possible the facts of the current situation and its impact on the business in the short and long term.

- Set your priorities as expressed above, and be very clear about what you want to achieve.

- Develop a crisis plan that will tackle those priorities with very specific decisions that are quantifiable and time-sensitive. The leader should consolidate the decision-making authority to protect the plan, and some information can be on a need-to-know basis as it might impact some of the team members. Making decisions amid uncertainty is difficult, but you have to work with the facts at hand and your intuition to make the call.

- Promote deliberate calm, positivity, and psychological safety to your teams who are working in a tense environment so they can discuss the situation openly through healthy debate and help you with solutions. Projecting confidence adds to your credibility and unites the teams behind you.

- Establish and assign duties to the team members as needed and as they fit the plan in progress. Some managers might assume new roles not related to their job description but based on their capabilities. It is in your hands to empower the right people to make some crisis response decisions as needed under your guidance.

- You should pause every now and then to assess new information that might impact your plan and modify your decisions based on it. Once you reach a decision, you must act with resolve and decisiveness to build confidence.

- Remember to always treat human tragedy as a first priority. The leader has a vital role in making a positive difference in people's lives. You should acknowledge the personal and professional challenges your employees and their families are experiencing during the crisis. Empathy is a great attribute in a leader's character, and you should keep an ongoing dialogue with your team. A crisis is the time when you have to reach out to all members of your team and stay connected, whether physically or via online meetings. They will be hungry to hear from the leader to understand the situation and remain calm. Maintain transparency and provide frequent updates; be clear about what you know and what you don't know.

Crisis times are the real test for a leader and will show their true character. Keep the faith, lead your team.

Millennial Talk

Old and New Ways

Millennial Talk

Life is changing very fast, and modern-day technologies have impacted our lives and the way we do things. It also created a new generation, a new breed of young people (mostly born between 1980 and 2000) who think and do things in a very different way than in the old days. These people are called "Millennials." They are very comfortable with the use of new technologies and social media.

What We Think

Many of us "Old Timers" believe Millennials were not raised on the same ethics and basics that we were taught for years. We think they don't have enough experience to accomplish what we have done. They behave differently, they speak differently, and they attack our principles and beliefs. We can't even agree with them on many things, and yet we have them in our society, and we have to deal with them. Our belief is that the Millennials were not raised the same as older generations due to modern life technologies and open communication throughout the world with massive social media platforms.

They take things for granted and don't really understand and appreciate how we got here (or that is what we think). We believe they are confused, and we regret that we did not raise them well like in the good old days.

"It is mission impossible!"

What They Think

On the other hand, Millennials look at us and consider us old-style people who are not open-minded and not able to see the possibilities of a brighter future due to our mental limitations and our non-willingness to change our old ways, which we have learned for years. They want to change how we do things, and they are forcing us to accept it. They are not emotionally attached to us like we were to our families. They can't wait for things to come; they want them now. They are becoming a big part of our society, and their target is to do things in their new ways to have a better future while we resist.

"It is mission impossible!"

What's To Be Done

You see, we are in a big dilemma. *Old or young, which works better? Old ways or new ways?*

A difficult formula of old and new generations battling for survival. In your organization or even within your family, you are also faced with the same encounters, and you have a good mix of both generations under the same roof.

The fact is, to this date in our lives, both generations still have a lot to offer, and each one needs the other. By now, millennials made up half of the work force around the world. We can and should integrate the unique gifts this group has to offer. The older generation needs fresh ideas out of the box, which Millennials can offer, but they also need guidance on the basics and wisdom, which we can offer. You, as a successful leader, have to manage both to achieve your desired goals. Whether you are a Millennial or an older generation, you still need to deal with both.

We agree that the future of this earth is really in the hands of youth, and they have a lot of energy to offer. If we just know how to direct and use this energy, if we just know how to accept change and try new ways, this will allow for new results that, for sure, we did not think of.

So how can we integrate with Millennials in the workplace to achieve our goals?

Integration Phase

- Millennials are persistent and don't usually stop at the first solution, so make sure you have an open mind and listen to their suggestions carefully, as they want to do things in an unconventional way.

- Be open to change and try new ways. They can easily find information and share new perspectives that you did not know about.

- Increase your use of technology when possible, and if you are not tech savvy, you need to learn fast. You can connect with them faster through various platforms, even though they do like face-to-face conversations, but you will relate better if you speak their language.

- Definitely increase your usage of social media at work by creating chat groups. Some leaders are still reluctant to do this, which impacts their communication. Millennials depend on the internet and social media for fast results and to get the job done, so make sure you are on board.

All my kids are Millennials, and I have worked hard in the past years to level with them in many ways and to close the gap between my generation and their generation. I love it when they say, "You are a cool dad and can relate to us". Social media, in fact, helped me stay connected to them and relate better to their needs and beliefs.

If you show Millennials that you care about them and their ideas, they will also open up to you and listen to your advice on many occasions. Yes, they can be wrong at times, as we are, but they have more courage to try new things that we are afraid to try.

"So, go on and find the Millennial in you."

I must not forget to mention that after millennials comes a new generation, "Gen Z," or so-called "Zoomers," who are very reliant on the internet and more diversified than previous generations.

They were born between 2000 and 2010 and will soon also be a big part of our business lives.

We need to keep learning and adapting in order to work well with all generations. After all, they are the future of the world.

Guest Engagement

Marketing

Guests Engagement

For your business to succeed, guest engagement is a key factor. Sales efforts alone cannot do the trick, but with proper service standards, the branding of your product, and then introducing it to the world through marketing, you can reach your target audience and achieve your goals.

Engagement means you are connected to your guests by all means on an ongoing basis. You are continuously delivering your message, information, and promotions to the right audience who desire your product, while at the same time receiving their feedback to adjust your services and ultimately responding to it. When an executive is fully committed to the above, we call him "fully engaged."

Marketing is a dynamic field that is evolving very fast and, in this day and age of technology, is even moving at light speed. One important channel of engagement is social media, where it has become a key factor in our day-to-day communication and reaching out to a vast majority of guests. It impacts your brand's perception and your profits.

As an executive, you should first identify the target audience that you want to communicate with, and you must go deeper to understand the persona of these clients. This means you must know their nationalities, age groups, social status, income levels, etc. This is called targeted marketing, as you don't want to waste your efforts and money on those who are not interested in your product.

The key area of engagement is "social media marketing" also known as digital marketing or e-marketing. These channels have in recent years outpaced the historical methods of advertising through newspapers and magazines. Further, they are relatively cheaper and reach far more people, especially your target audience.

The ability to adapt and evolve "digital strategy" has become essential to increasing profits as affluent travelers have been empowered with choices. Expectations are changing when it comes to showcasing authenticity, the digital user experience, and the seamless integration of mobile into every step of the traveler's journey.

To maintain their competitive edge, luxury hoteliers must be flexible and forward-thinking in their digital approach.

Visual contents are crucial and include video, pictures, emails, websites, blogs, and other visual media. People don't buy what you do; they buy why you do it and how it makes them feel. These days, many platforms include your target audience, such as Facebook, Instagram, WhatsApp, Twitter, and others. You must invest time in UGC (user-generated content), which means digital content created, uploaded, and shared publicly online by customers through pictures, videos, blog posts, discussion boards, product or service reviews, comments, tweets, etc.

The following are some steps to help you focus your efforts to get best results;

Awareness Stage

Create branded content that reaches and engages with the audience and customers. Prepare your content of videos, pictures, and promotions that you want to share very thoroughly. A good investment is needed in this matter to make sure it is done professionally.

Reach

Reach your audience through search engines, social networks, publishers, and influencers.

You must contract with a digital marketing agency and a social marketing agency that will facilitate this task for you. They will review your content and post it appropriately through the various channels. The agency will guide you to the best timing of posts and channels.

Possible topics, depending on your business, can include:

- Engagement-oriented with facts and surveys, property pictures, and travel tips.
- Destination-oriented holidays and attractions
- Hotel news on events, media coverage, upgrades, and other highlights.
- User-generated content such as guest reviews, pictures, stories, special events, new menus, etc.
- Website content includes amenities, room pages, newsletters, packages, catering, blogs, loyalty

programs, and other discount information.

- Videos for product or guest interviews, testimonials, or a hotel minute weekly update.

- Weekly hashtags creating one for each day of the week to promote something.

- Contests and giveaways to create customer engagement.

Act

Act to be worth finding via a clear customer journey and a content hub that is relevant and inspirational through a website, blog, email, and interactive tool.

Convert

Convert the business through e-commerce and other CRM channels to generate profits. So, make sure your pricing strategy, after considering your competitive set, is correct with the right values to ensure sales are moving in the right direction to convert into revenues and profits.

Engage

Engage with your customers; they are the key to reviews, social media marketing, repeat sales, and referrals.

Your agency will generate monthly reports that will show your reach to clients and how many people engage with your digital or social media marketing. Your number of followers and likes is a key indicator of your performance.

Manage Response

Last but not least, you must continuously engage with your clients by replying to their comments and feedback. Management response is crucial to achieving 100% on all channels. Assess their reviews and their ideas, and reply promptly to every comment. It shows your guests that you care and also shows the world how you are engaged with clients. These reviews and your replies have a huge impact on your volume of business.

One not to forget is your engagement with your in-house guests. Those, when handled properly, will pass the message to thousands of others and could be your future repeat guests. Your guests will be the most critical and will give you the most honest feedback about your business.

Not only will you encounter happy guests but you will also face some complaints. Once you know what went wrong, it is your opportunity to correct it to avoid future complaints.

It is key that we listen to those guests carefully, empathize with them, apologize for their feelings, and most importantly, react with corrective measures.

Successful leaders follow the above steps and turn the situation around in their favor.

"A complaint is an opportunity to win a customer for life."

Business Development

Sales

Business Development

You probably know that every employee in your organization is a salesperson, and this is very true. Nowadays, we need everyone's efforts to infiltrate busy and difficult markets in a highly competitive world.

If you instill this notion in your team's mind from day one as an integral part of their duties, you will have a greater impact on increasing your revenue streams.

Sales is Science

It requires great leadership skills, creativity, and determination. The director of business development or director of sales, along with the general manager, are the key drivers of sales strategies to achieve budget revenues. The sales process starts with a basic understanding of the sources of your business, including which segments and which feeder markets. This can be determined by thorough market research in your city and a close study of your potential competitors. You need clarity about what you are up against.

During the development of your business plan for the hotel,

you will have already dissected this in detail during the planning stage and have a clear vision of your target business mix. It is important to understand that this process is very methodical and not random.

"You should have clarity on the who, what, where, when, and how in every step of the sales process. "

Business Plan

Your business plan is your road map, which guides every decision you make. Once you have completed your market research analysis and determined your feeder markets and segments, you are ready to dig deeper into how to reach those clients. You should have a clear idea of the "persona" of the clients who you seek for your product in order to target those clients through direct sales or marketing. The technology enabled us to reach those specific clients through various channels, which will save you time and money.

Your potential revenues are then formulated for each segment to arrive at your total budget revenues. So much goes into this process to breakdown the various elements of your selling packages for each segment, along with determining the best channel to reach it, all according to your competitive set study and the set targets. Of course, you will list your top 10 target companies, groups, organizations, or entities for each segment, and you will have clarity on who exactly you want to go after. Deciding the budget occupancy and the average room rate is dependent on your target positioning in the market, which is determined according to your quality of product and service levels.

The business plan will also highlight details of the "selling strategies" for each of your segments and the required channels to reach them. In order to determine a suitable selling strategy, you need to master the format of your communication tools, engagement targets, indoor and outdoor activities, seasonality calendars, and pricing structure for each segment or market.

Sales Plan Activities

Once the goals for the budget and your strategies are clear, you will move on to the next stage of breaking down your strategies into a very detailed sales plan that includes every possible activity. This will also include assigning targets to each sales manager, against which his productivity will be measured. The sales plan has two major channels from which it is driven. The B2B "Business to Business" channels and the B2C "Business to Client" channels, where activities vary based on targeted audience, seasonality calendars, clientele profiles, and the most important factor, which is the decision-making influencer.

"B2B" segment activities begin by networking with potential clients and partners. Personal business relationship development is the key to a successful long-term deal. In addition, active searching and qualifying of new accounts through various tools is key to widening your business potential. Key account management activities include calls, visits, social events, and promotions, which keep the clients engaged, loyal, and up-to-date.

Further attending exhibitions related to your business is key to staying connected to your "B2B" segment.

"B2C" deals directly with buyers or guests who plan to stay at your hotel through personal contact, emails, your website, and other channels such as offline or online travel agencies that display your services directly to clients.

Public engagement and marketing activities, followed by a strong service reputation through various platforms, drive the success of this segment. The activities focus mainly on personal lifestyle experiences expressed through hosting public figures, media influences, advertisements, and press events at the property.

Based on the planned activities, it requires follow-up on a daily, weekly, monthly, or annual basis, "such as contracting trips." Each team member is required to report and upload his activities to the system on a daily basis to be reviewed by the director, who will ensure everyone is on target as planned. Smart Directors of Sales will further assign activities to other managers at the hotel who will help in either relationship building or prospecting for new business.

A sales blitz to prospect new business in the immediate

market is one activity that requires the involvement of as many managers as possible to cover a wide area.

Managing the Team

You cannot convince clients of your product if you don't know it well and are convinced yourself. The first step in managing your sales team is to ensure their "product knowledge." Most importantly, they have to believe in it and have confidence in what they are selling. This will be conveyed in every encounter they have with clients and is a key driver for securing deals.

Make sure that everyone involved in the sales process has attended proper orientation for your product as well as your selling strategies and techniques so everyone speaks the same language and portrays the right image.

"Tracking the activities

carried out to achieve the strategies,

is a key measurement of where you are headed."

Managing the sales team is of great importance throughout the sales process. Each manager should have his own targets set well in advance and a clear set of activities outlined for him to reach those clients. This is where many leaders fail when they don't follow the process to know where they stand and to reinforce the effectiveness of the sales managers. They need to constantly and regularly convert their efforts into revenue streams. Tracking their productivity on a monthly basis is key to making the needed adjustments to ensure conversions and closing deals.

The director should acknowledge his team's strengths and weaknesses before assigning the activities and ensure that the team itself understands that they complement each other in the field. While the incentive plan is built based on each sales manager's productivity, a good portion is also built based on the team's productivity.

The leader is responsible for ensuring a high level of communication between the team itself, their management, peers, clients, and prospects.

It all begins with "building trust" and "cooperation" from the very early stages between the team members.

"One for all and all for one."

Modern management styles avoid micro-management, especially with new generations such as "Millennials." Give space, freedom, high responsibility, and authority to every member to perform his selling activities within the organization's selling strategies. They should understand the roots of the strategies built and created by the management. The leader keeps a close eye and redirects when needed.

"Leaders trust but verify."

Last but not least, keeping your team fully engaged and well informed is key to building their trust and confidence to achieve great heights.

Sales Team Characteristics

Depending on the strength of your sales team, you should pay very special attention to their self-confidence, presentation skills, and negotiation skills.

This is needed in every step, and you should invest time and money to flourish with these skills.

They represent you, your organization, and your image. What they portray to the market impacts you directly. Make sure you use the latest technology gadgets available for them to use on the road to conduct presentations of your products and have immediate access to all the information they need.

Revenue Management and Pricing

It is a key factor that will impact the sales team's efforts. The general manager heading the revenue committee, along with the director of sales, revenue manager, reservation manager, and director of finance, make the collective decisions required for the property pricing, both static and dynamic.

"Establishing clear guidelines for pricing

and ample market knowledge,

will positively impact your sales drive."

In this fast-moving world, "demand and supply" change by the minute, and you should be on top of your game, adjusting your pricing and strategies based on both for all segments. This will allow maximum returns and conversions. You should assess your decisions on a weekly basis to ensure you are on track.

Usually, when the Revenue Manager and the Director of Sales are in conflict over the pricing decision, this is a healthy sign, and you as a leader must balance between the two to reach a good decision that is beneficial to the organization and aligned with your short- and long-term goals for hotel positioning.

There could be many ways to reach sales targets, whether based on business volume or on rate. It should be clear where you stand in every decision based on your positioning statement, which you have included in the business plan. Positioning is critical to your product image as well as the pricing. Too many discounts, and you might end up competing with another set of competitors who don't match your product and service. Too much rate can put you out of the competition for your hotel set.

The decisions you make on a daily basis will impact your revenues and are also dependent on the dynamics of the market. There are many tools for revenue management to monitor your performance and that of the market, so make sure you take advantage of it.

Food for Thought

Food and Beverage

Food for Thought

Food for thought, it's time to shed light on a key department such as "Food & Beverage." It has become the heart and soul of many successful hotels. Depending on your hotel category, you will most likely have some sort of F&B offerings for your guests. Here I share with you some of the important thoughts on how you should approach this and what important factors you should look for.

As previously mentioned, developing your team is essential to your success, particularly in the food and beverage division. Whether or not you have prior experience in this field, you must appoint competent managers for both the kitchen and the service. Many hotels compete in this area to generate revenue, and there is a lot of work to be done to make this department successful.

In certain situations, even more so than room revenues, food and beverage can be the hotel's primary source of income. It may also affect how much money you make from rooms by drawing in repeat business from people who come to stay at your hotel specifically because of your outlets.

As a leader in the F&B department, you have a lot of priorities to take into account. So, you know what to expect, let's take it one step at a time.

Food and Beverage Concepts

The first key is your understanding of your outlet's concepts. Each outlet is different and targets certain clients in-house or outside. Usually, the outlet concept is prepared for you by an expert prior to the opening of the hotel who has conducted detailed market research before arriving at this concept. In order for this concept to work and be successful, it has to be implemented as per the guidelines of the founders. The concept should clearly explain every detail of the outlet, from setup, décor, menus, ambiance, music, uniforms, service standards, presentations, and other details.

The concept details that are set will determine and impact any decisions you need to make. So, first things first, go ahead and review and have a full understanding of your outlet concept.

You should determine if it is fully implemented as per the original plan and if the outlet is successful or not,

depending on its profitability and the production of the desired results. If you feel the concept is not fully implemented as per the plan, then this is the first thing to do by involving both your executive chef and the director of F&B, who should also understand well what is expected.

This does not mean we have to stay with the same concept for ever; sometimes things don't work and you have to make adjustments. These adjustments within the boundaries of the concept are totally acceptable, and they are based on market and guest feedback on certain elements of the concept. You must not make these decisions alone and should consult both at the corporate level and at the hotel level, and in some cases, involve owners.

Outlet performance

It is super important, and you should receive detailed data for each outlet separately showing the number of covers achieved per meal and the average check.

Not only this, but you should review in detail the reports highlighting the most popular items in that venue, as well as your guest feedback.

Once you have reviewed your concept and made sure all its attributes are followed 100% in terms of food quality, food presentation, and food service, and you have reached the conclusion that you are very satisfied with what you see, the next step is to look at your marketing schemes.

Marketing and advertising

You see, restaurants can be successful with word of mouth, as they usually say, but nowadays, with so much competition you cannot do it without marketing and advertising.

"If people don't know about what you offer,

they will not come."

It is that simple, and your goal is to reach as many clients as possible and convince them to try your products and services.

Your collateral is the first of many tasks involved in

marketing. Anywhere you display or market your product—in hotel rooms, on menus in restaurants, in public spaces, on digital screens, or on websites—you have to make sure it is of the highest caliber, visually appealing, accurate, and compliant with your company's style guidelines.

Social media is another major area of focus for marketing in order to promote, raise awareness, and generate demand. It is now the most popular way to connect with clients, and nearly everyone uses it to select his favorite food and beverage options. Your marketing manager, your team, and the marketing firm that manages your social media accounts should all be highly focused on this topic.

Everything you want to promote and advertise needs to be planned out for the upcoming quarter and must be decided upon in advance. If this is not the case, you ought to begin right away. Effective leaders anticipate needs and anticipate the future before others do. Actually, every outlet ought to have a year-round calendar that includes noteworthy occasions, events, and exclusive deals.

Guest Feedback

Monitoring "guest feedback" on all channels for your F&B outlets is crucial to understanding your performance, and it is equally important to reply to guests' feedback, when possible, to create engagement.

You will learn a lot from the guests' comments, and replying to them constantly will keep you connected.

Consistency

It is another very important topic when it comes to the F&B department. You must ensure you deliver what you promise in a consistent manner. This is done through hard work and constant auditing and monitoring of your product and service. You should regularly visit all your outlets without notice and try the food and service by yourself to ensure the standards of service and food quality you desire are met. Your executive chef plays a great role in ensuring food quality and consistency. You should support him to have the right products to obtain the desired recipes.

Service Concept

Some other important factors to consider are

"Service Standards Sequence" based on the outlet concept, followed by "Speed of Service," and most importantly, your "Guest Engagement." Service sequence is important and depends on the outlet concept, whether it is fine dining or casual.

Experienced clients have high expectations for some of the service protocols that should be in place for such outlets. You have to ensure your team is following the operational standards set in place and the desired service protocol and sequence.

Another factor is that the lack of "speed of service" aggravates customers more than anything else. This is your real test of how well your kitchen and staff can produce the same caliber food within the allotted time when your venue gets busy. Competent chefs schedule their workload in advance.

Finally, but just as importantly, "Guest Engagement" throughout the whole dining experience has an impact on the guest's perception in numerous ways. The interaction of your staff is what makes the experience complete, in addition to the taste of the food, which is extremely important.

Pay close attention to the staff hygiene, restaurant cleanliness, and welcoming and seating experiences. These all affect how happy your visitors are.

Eating is enjoyable and always has a backstory. It is important that your staff be trained to engage in conversation with visitors, particularly when relating tales about the provenance, methods of preparation, and other details of your food. Periodically, your chef can interact with guests by being interactive on the floor. They wish to meet the hero who made their favorite dish.

Creativity

What sets the best apart from the rest are their inventive elements of surprise. Their guests are left in awe as they always have something new to offer. Unexpectedly pleasant surprises go a long way. Acknowledging a guest's special occasion or even providing a free sample of a new item can greatly enhance the guest experience and strengthen the relationship.

A clever chef will always prepare a live action dish for their guests, which makes a big impression. There are numerous applications for creativity, including menu presentation.

Value for money

So how do you price this experience? Sometimes you visit different restaurants that offer similar food menus, but one is more expensive than the other. Guess Why? It is not only the quality of the food served but also the overall experience the guests go through while spending time at your venue.

"You need to stay ahead of the competition

by knowing your competition well."

It is essential that you regularly survey your competitors to stay abreast of market trends, compare pricing and products, and learn about their offerings. In order to stay ahead of the curve in the ever-evolving food and beverage industry, it is imperative that new and innovative ideas are consistently implemented.

The cost of the food is only one factor that affects how much to charge for your product; other overhead costs also play a role. The value of your offerings is determined by various factors such as ambiance, décor, music, style of service, entertainment, live food corners, and much more, which make guests willing to pay extra for unique experiences.

The kitchen Story

Everyone knows that the restaurant experience starts with the kitchen story since the core of the journey is about food, headed by an experienced chef and a talented team. The kitchen story has many critical stages, starting with purchasing of the right quality product and ending with delivery of your food delights to the end user.

Purchasing and Receiving

You should regularly receive the high-quality products you want if your system is operating effectively. To guarantee the quality and consistency of the products, you should work with your chef to determine what grade level of goods you require for each outlet. Your chef or his assistant should be present at all times during the receiving process.

They will make sure that hygienic and safety protocols are followed when it comes to packaging and unpacking, and they will accept or reject some of the products based on expectations. These actions will guarantee a consistent and high-quality product.

A good system of ordering procedures must be in place, along with minimum and maximum stock counts, to ensure timely delivery of products.

As a leader, you should always ensure that this is done correctly. You should also try to find time during your hectic day to visit this process. There are a lot of things that could go wrong and affect the safety and quality of your food.

Food safety and hygiene audits

Nowadays, it is required to hire a hygiene consultant who will conduct monthly visits to audit your process and usually highlight any deficiencies you may have. These audits are your basis for starting and obtaining the "HACCP" certification ("Hazard Analysis Critical Control Point"), which most hotels are seeking.

You need to become very familiar with such audit reports. Don't just settle for the executive report; make sure you dissect the details with your food and beverage team to understand the process and what needs to be done. It is a very valuable resource for you to understand how your kitchen teams are performing and their level of hygiene.

Before conducting business or sending clients to the hotel, tour operators and other organizations that work with your establishment frequently ask to see a copy of this audit to ensure that you are handling food in a hygienic and safe manner for the benefit of their patrons. Make it a culture in your hotel because, as you will recall, it takes a whole team to keep this cycle going.

Kitchen Tour

How is your kitchen looking? Is it clean and well-maintained?

Take a tour of the kitchen regularly to ensure that it simply shines at all times. Even during the busiest times, good chefs keep the kitchen well maintained during their shifts.

This is a sign of a good hygiene culture within your teams. Start with the general cleanliness of the kitchen surfaces, followed by a deep look into hoods, equipment, and storage units.

Take a look at your team to see if they are wearing their appropriate uniform, including "aprons, hair nets, and gloves." If yes, it's a good indication of good practices, and if not, act quickly to get them into this habit.

A clean and proper uniform is a good indication for the rest of the operation.

Food Storage

Another important element is checking your food storage procedures ("frozen, cooled, or dried"), where many things can go wrong and impact your quality.

A quick look around your storage areas can tell the whole story. Critical things to look for include freezer separations, temperatures, labels with preparation and expiration dates, proper packing, etc. "Refer to your hygiene company audit report for a detailed list." This step is important to avoid several municipal fines during inspections.

Recipes and food presentation

They play a huge role in the success of the restaurant. Make sure you review this with your F&B team from time to time. The recipe card for each dish, which should also include a picture of the final look of the dish, must be followed at all times and should be accessible to all cooks. It ensures consistency in both the quality and quantity of the product and the desired look and feel.

Food Waste

Last but not least, your chef plays a great role in minimizing food waste to control costs, especially in buffet-style outlets, by following a set of guidelines.

As a leader, following these steps regularly will give you confidence in your kitchen's "hygiene and quality" and will make you prouder of what you offer to your clients.

"Cooking is a passion,
and when done with love and care,
it can create an amazing experience."

People Engagement

Recruitment and Retention

People Engagement

Typically known as "Human Resources," now referred to as "People Engagement," It is not only a matter of recruiting the right employees; the continued engagement with them is what counts.

This department is very critical to instilling the culture of the organization and sustaining the business long-term through manpower to achieve the company goals.

"It is manpower that makes any organization successful."

Let us explore further the various key aspects of "people engagement" and what you have to focus on as a leader in your organization to capitalize on your most important asset, the employees.

"It is crucial to stay fully engaged with your guests;

it is equally important to stay fully engaged

with your employees."

Recruitment Process

One of the most important functions in the People Engagement department is "recruitment" to ensure hiring the right employees, retaining them, and making sure they are performing the tasks for which you hired them at sustainable high productivity levels. You need to establish very clear search criteria guidelines for each job role, with detailed job descriptions and a set of pre-requisites for each role. Prerequisites can include years of experience, a particular skill, a particular knowledge of a system, etc.

Establishing such guidelines will assist your PE team in filtering, screening, and finding the right employees who match the desired job role. Whether you recruit through your own website, direct applications, or through a third-party recruitment agency, having these clear expectations will ensure you find the right caliber you are looking for. The next important and critical step is the interview process, which you should not take lightly.

The Interview

The candidate who has been screened by the PE department and was found to have met all the pre-requisites and set criteria for the job role is invited to the next stage of the process, which is "the interview," and can be conducted by phone, video conference, or in person. Conducting an interview has many techniques that allow you to determine the suitability of the candidate.

Perceiving the candidate correctly and understanding his capabilities and background experience during an interview is such an important matter. You have to watch carefully for each move, posture, and answer given by the candidate, which can give you many signals pertaining to his behavior and true background experience.

You must be prepared for the interview and have thoroughly reviewed the resume and supporting documents. The meeting should be structured to cover many aspects, starting with personal traits and ending with detailed technical questions relating to the job role. Pay special attention to the candidate's attitude signals during the interview process.

Once you have completed the interview process, make sure you obtain a thorough "reference check" for the employee you desire to hire. Many managers fail to take this step and have to live with the consequences in the future. Many companies use a third-party "online assessment," which gives you an idea of the employee's personal traits. This has proven to be very valuable and gives a good indication of the employees' long-term prospects. If this is available to you, it should definitely be applied for, especially for supervisory and managerial roles. While this assessment should not be used as the basis for the decision to hire such a candidate, it will highlight some concerns about the candidate's character, which you can monitor closely during the probation period to make a good assessment.

Many candidates can fool you during the interview process, and taking your time and doing an extra thorough investigation can save you from high turnover rates at a later stage.

Orientation

Once your employee is on board, you should give utmost importance to the orientation "on board" process, which will bring him awareness of the vision and values of your company. If you want him to be synchronized with other team members, don't throw him on the floor until this step is completed.

The employee must understand clearly what is expected of him to perform his duties and work with the team under a common vision.

You need to keep a close eye on his performance during the probation period, which usually lasts 90 days. You should receive a biweekly update from his department head during this period so you can make a final assessment within 60 days if you hired the right candidate or not.

Brand Image

The PE department is also responsible for parts of the brand image by ensuring the values and culture are instilled in your team members, as well as enforcing other standards such as uniforms, nametags, etc. Make sure, as a leader, you enforce those standards without any deviation.

Uniform design is part of your brand image and very important to convey the right message to your guests, of who you are.

Engagement

Now comes your role as a leader for continuous engagement with your employees. You don't want to leave anyone behind; you want to be reachable, approachable, and well informed of their concerns and well-being.

Engagement with your employees means you have to lead from the front and be regularly visible in the operation, directing and enforcing policies and procedures. Engagement means listening to their concerns and feedback, which can be done through regular meetings with your department heads to discuss employee issues or conducting town halls regularly to hear directly from the employees. Engagement means continuous care for the employee's well-being in terms of living standards and other related benefits.

As a leader, you must ensure that policies and procedures are enforced and applied fairly to all members of your team, with no favoritism. Your team looks up to you as the one who leads by example, and they are hungry for fair treatment and equality.

Employee Satisfaction

You should also engage with them through a neutral third party to get their honest feedback.

This is usually done through employee surveys, the best of which is online employee feedback software, which can engage with them on a 24/7 basis.

Employees who feel cared for usually go the extra mile and will support you even more in times of need. The more you care, the more you will ensure high employee satisfaction, increase productivity, and reduce turnover.

Employee Well-being

In addition, you should give great attention to your employees' housing, meals, and medical treatment (for those hotels that are responsible for accommodating employees). If they sleep well, eat well, and remain healthy, they will be happy and produce more.

The well-being of employees also involves the activities that you can engage them in during their spare time, whether sports or community activities, which are necessary to maintain their mental state of mind and physical health.

Manning Guide

Do you have the right manpower? Do you have the right caliber? Those are questions that you should answer.

Having the correct manpower and the right caliber will have a great impact on productivity. You can do more with fewer employees, get high-quality end results, and achieve consistency.

Depending on the level of service you offer at your business, this is determined by your budget. Many times, businesses are dependent on the outsourcing of employees due to business level fluctuations. This practice is a necessary evil but will impact your service and consistency. You must make extra effort to train those employees on the basic tasks required of them and to keep them monitored at all times.

Local Laws

With the help of your people engagement manager, as a leader, you must be kept informed of your country's local labor laws and have a good grip on the dos and don'ts. You need to make sure you follow the law fully and avoid any labor office complaints, which could cost you fines. Having an open-door policy and fair treatment will definitely minimize such a risk.

Having a correct and fair salary scale in your organization is one way to reduce complaints. This is usually governed by your company's policies and procedures, which you should adhere to closely.

Summary

The formula for people's engagement is to care, communicate, and coordinate. Show them you care by meeting and listening to them; have continuous dialogue, when possible, through various channels; and, on an ongoing basis, coordinate all their ideas and needs with your department heads to alleviate their concerns.

"You should be aware at all times of the climate of your hotel in terms of equality, integrity, respect, care, credibility, identity, and fellowship."

Live and Learn

Learning and Development

Live and Learn

As expressed earlier, "knowledge" is an integral part of success; without it, you will not achieve your goals. It is essential that you understand that learning is the heart of the organization and should be available to all members equally.

When you increase the knowledge levels of your employees, it means improving service, consistency, self-esteem, and everyone's ability to perform their duties as expected. Not only this, but taking an interest in the development of your team will create a sense of belonging and high motivation.

> *"Learning and development*
> *should be instilled*
> *as part of the culture in your organization."*

So how should you go about it? Each member has a different learning curve, which you should assess. Preparing a global training plan for your business requires a full understanding of the needs of each employee and the needs of the organization, along with the required goals.

Learning and Development Plan

- Define your overall objectives based on your business plan and your company directives.

- Complete a training needs analysis based on your objectives. A need analysis report should be completed for each employee separately to understand his level of learning and what he requires to perform and meet your objectives. Set all the training topics very carefully to ensure maximum returns.

- Use the guest feedback through all available channels to design specific trainings related to the guests' comments and observations.

- Compile a training plan that is outlined for daily, monthly, quarterly, and annual targets.

- The training plan must be conclusive and identify all the topics and channels to be used. Use all the resources available and make sure you have a good balance. A goal number of training hours must be set by the department and by the employee.

- Establish a measurement tool for all your training to quantify your accomplishments and ensure effectiveness. Measurements can be end results, self-audits, performance scores, etc.

- Track your achievements throughout the year on a monthly basis. Quiet often, we do a lot of work, but we don't track what we do. This is a huge mistake made by many. All activities must be documented and tracked on a daily basis. A record must be kept daily of who attended the training, what they learned, and their assessment of their comprehension of the topic.

- Finally, reporting on all of the above in a professional, concise presentation will show your superior how much effort you have put into the development of your teams in a professional manner to reach your goals.

Training Channels

- On-the-job training focuses on technical and customer interactions. This type of training is usually conducted by the department expert or the designated trainer of the department, who should be highly skilled and trained by your training manager to be able to teach others.

- Off-the-job training, usually classroom-style, is usually conducted by your training manager and supported at times by department heads and the general manager. Also, classroom-style training can include outside speakers and influencers who can impact your teams.

- E-Learning using the various available online software learning tools, with which most probably your organization is contracted, targets certain elements by department according to your needs.

- Attending webinars with experts is another venue for training that should be considered.

- Schedule seminars with a third-party professional trainer to teach specific topics.

- School training, as some of your job needs might require that some of the members have to attend courses in schools, colleges, or educational centers, or even to attend certain leadership or specific conferences to raise their skills.

Obviously, one of the key elements in the success of your learning and development are the subjects and information you are feeding to your team. Every topic and every step must be well written and documented. Every procedure being taught must be outlined and signed by each employee after the session is complete.

If you focus on training your employees consistently, you will raise their level of knowledge and their self-esteem, and for sure, you will get a huge return on investment in terms of achieving your goals. In addition, developing your managers is a huge part of your responsibility to prepare them for the next level.

If you take care of the managers, they will take care of the employees, who in turn will take care of the guests. a very simple formula that has proven successful over the years.

"If you care, they will care."

High Tech

Technology

High Tech

Technology has evolved and advanced in recent years to unprecedented levels, infiltrating our lives in many aspects and continue to play a huge role in our business delivery and success. Technology has made many things deemed impossible possible and connected the entire world in ways never thought of. Business nowadays moves at light speed, and for you to be a successful leader, you have to get on board.

Technology has surely made our lives easier in many ways, but some still consider it a burden that carries a huge investment cost. Hotel business has become technology-dependent in every aspect of the operation, and it is crucial that you, as a leader, embrace the use of technology to enhance the operations and ultimately positively impact your top margins.

"Applying the right technology is important to obtain the desired results and return on investment. "

Technology Guidelines

Most companies have established parameters and

guidelines for the use of technology and systems, which is probably the case in your hotel. Those guidelines, along with operating standards, should be your reference for the systems to be installed and used for every function in the operation.

Keep in mind that technology is changing fast, and it is imperative that you keep up with it or it will become a huge investment burden that you might not be able to afford. Along with your company and your information technology manager, you should assess your needs according to allocated budgets. Your IT manager and his team are vital employees in your organization, whom you should choose very carefully. Their actions can save or cost you thousands in the long run.

Applying Technology

Technology is divided into several groups of hardware and software according to its use in the hotel business: "Infrastructure and Communication Systems," "Front and Back of House Operational Systems," and "Interactive Systems."

"Infrastructure and communication systems" include the servers, computers, and operating systems that are the core of your hotel operations. It's the main frame, which hosts all your data and interfaces with the various other systems. Communication systems allow for global networking and connectivity between systems and the outside world.

"Operational systems" front and back of house are critical to performing your daily tasks and enhancing customer satisfaction. They include hardware and software that is interfaced to your main frame. Each department has a specific system to perform the duties pertaining to the department in a fast and efficient manner, which can save time and money.

Those systems include front office operations for room inventory management, reservations, check-in and check-out, food and beverage, material control, accounting, and catering, to name a few. They are used by the employees to serve the guests in a fast and efficient manner and have immediate access to guest history information, profiles, and other statistics.

In addition, the advanced Building Management System ("BMS") will assist you in monitoring and controlling most electromechanical equipment in the hotel so you can better maintain the asset and save energy and time.

"Interactive systems" are the third group, which has become a huge necessity and distinguishes one hotel service standard from another. This group is composed of systems and software used directly by guests, such as Internet access, interactive TV, Internet protocol telephones, USB charging, and other guest room management systems.

"Internet speed and Wi-Fi coverage are two of the most important elements, impacting guest satisfaction."

Guests depend on these features to interact with your team and your organization. It is an opportunity for you to show what you offer. Their expectations in this new digital world are extremely high when it comes to connectivity.

You should give this matter the highest priority and monitor the guest feedback carefully.

This third group also includes all the possible systems that interface directly with guests via online applications, phone applications, and other means. Recently, new technologies have allowed guests to self-check in via mobile devices, even giving room access through the same.

Pay attention to your visibility and connectivity online with the world outside. Everyone finds what they are looking for online, and having the latest technology and connectivity software will allow you to stay engaged, such as with your reservation systems and hotel website.

Last but not least, rest assured that there is a solution for everything you are looking for that will help you be more efficient in serving your guests, so make use of the technology and consult your IT expert.

Information Security

Securing hotel data and guest information is paramount to your success.

Setting up several layers of security and accessibility guidelines is important for the organization to protect its data. Your employees should be aware of such access rights and have signed on to them.

Whether you are a technology fan or not, you can't operate your business without it. Your success in managing complex operations depends on the investment you make in technology. Study carefully the return on investment "ROI" for each system you seek, as it impacts the top line, bottom line, or guest satisfaction.

In and Out

Rooms Division

In and Out

Offering accommodation is the core of our business so naturally Rooms division is the heart of the operation and in general the highest revenue generating department in most hotels. Understanding and monitoring the performance of the various teams is key to driving business with high customer satisfaction and maintaining high occupancy and rate levels to sustain profits.

"First impression is key to your business success."

The rooms division journey starts with the front office team extending guest warm welcome and first impressions that sets the tone throughout the stay. The arrival experience, as known to many, defines who you are and presents a glimpse of the quality of service and standards you offer to your clients. The roles of key members such as doorman, bellman and reception clerks are important in the process.

Arrival Experience

Guests arriving to your hotel after a long journey seek smiles, warmth and efficient fast check-in so they can reach to their final destination of their choice in rooms or suites.

The arrival experience has a great impact on customer satisfaction and building loyal repeat guests. Don't mis-understand me this is required by all teams in all departments throughout the hotel but is specifically crucial on first guest contact to set the stage. Customers are very sensitive to what we say and what we do to welcome them.

Equally, services offered during the guest stay through operator, concierge and guest relations are critical to complete the guest experience. Training of the entire front office teams is of high priority. Lack or delay of services can be a great source of complaints from guests which will impact the operation.

Check-in and Check-out

The main duties of the front office department focus on guest check-in and Check-out which must be smooth, quick and efficient. The use of systems and technology has made the process easier and ensures accurate guest records.

The team has various means to recognize loyal and repeat customers who should receive special treatment throughout their stay.

As a leader this should be your first stop on daily basis to stay well informed and review your daily arrivals of VIP and loyal guests who you should give personalized treatment in writing or in person.

Room Experience

Once situated in their room or suite the guests encounter their second part of the hotel journey. The cleanliness and hygiene standards you have in place will make or break your business. This is followed by the maintenance conditions. Now a days guests are very critical and if not satisfied will voice their opinions which will affect your business reputation and eventually profits.

Housekeeping is one of the labor-intensive and hard to manage departments in the hotel and holds the key to success. You must ensure to have a strong leadership in such department that can manage the process and the multiple cleaning projects in effective manner.

The housekeeping teams interact with your guests throughout their stay and have a huge role in making them comfortable and happy. Small touches during room cleaning make a big impact on personalizing guest stay and make them feel at home.

The products used for bed linen and toiletries are also an important element to guests' satisfaction and must be chosen carefully to ensure a good sleep and enjoyable guest experience. Housekeeping supervisors have a key role in this process and must be trained well. They are your eyes and they are responsible to report any deficiencies to the responsible department before the room is released.

Public Area

Housekeeping teams are also responsible for your public area cleanliness and upkeep. This includes as well the smell, flowers and ambiance. The team runs multiple projects during the week to maintain those areas at a high level of cleanliness.

Third party vendors can be sourced for special surface treatments such as building façade, marble floors, pest control, etc. High hygiene standards mean high guest satisfaction, high repeat guests and in turn high profits.

Laundry Experience

Quiet often hotels have their own laundry operations within the premises to clean linen, staff uniforms and guests' garments. This is an added value when done efficiently. But in some cases, this linen process is outsourced to a third party and extra care must be taken to ensure the quality standards are met. The housekeeping managers must focus on the process to avoid loss and damage of linen and other garments sent to the vendor.

Communication

For the rooms division department to operate well, communication is important between the teams. The tasks at hand require very high level of interaction almost on the hour to get the job done properly and most importantly on time to avoid delay in check ins and avoid guest complaints. The use of technology is paramount in this process and many hotels use various programs to do this.

The applications used ensure pertinent issues are reported promptly and tracked for timely resolution. You want to avoid out of order rooms to avoid loss of revenues.

Weekly rooms division meetings between the two department leaders and key managers are key to keeping the communication lines open and keeping you as a leader well informed of the important issues.

MEP

Engineering and Maintenance

MEP

Yes, you guessed it right, MEP stands for "mechanical, electrical and plumbing". MEP engineering is the science and art of planning, designing and managing the MEP systems of a building, mainly you engineering department.

So, why is this so important?

As a leader you are entrusted to not only the management of the business but also to maintain the assets and preserve or raise its value over the years. Engineering department have a huge responsibility in this regard and maintenance is key to sustaining business for long term and avoiding high expenses.

Hiring and retaining an experienced Chief engineer should be a top priority as this is a very specialized field requiring many years of education and experience. The duties required by this department are critical and directly impact important issues such as safety, sustainability and ultimately your asset value and profits.

There are many key priorities in managing the engineering department, one of which is the listing and tagging of your assets and systems information and historical data. This is quiet often not followed by many and in the long term leads to losses. Whether you have an automated system or not this step must be your starting point. All systems must be fully functional and in good working condition to operate your business without interruptions.

Preventive Maintenance

Preventive maintenance is the act of performing regularly scheduled maintenance activities to help prevent unexpected failures in the future. Put simply, it's about fixing things before they break. PPM or planned preventive maintenance is one of the most cumbersome tasks to complete and requires good project management skills to stay on top. The associated costs should be carefully budgeted to avoid surprises and ensure the maintenance goes on as scheduled.

Not following a good PPM program can cost you

money and will directly impact your bottom line. For example, if you don't maintain the FCU units (AC fan coil) in your guests' rooms, it will lead to motor being burned over time causing the room to be placed in out of order status which will lead to revenue loss and additional cost to fix the motor or purchase a new one. The same goes for all systems in the hotel which can break if not well maintained.

If you want to ensure guests stay comfortable there are four key areas of the hotel to prioritize;

- HVAC system maintenance
- Plumbing system maintenance
- Electrical system maintenance
- Lighting system maintenance

As a leader, ensure that your engineering team have the system in place and that you monitor their achievements on a monthly basis to ensure compliance.

Sustainability

In the broadest sense, sustainability refers to the ability to maintain or support a process continuously over time.

In business and policy contexts, sustainability seeks to prevent the depletion of natural or physical resources, so that they will remain available for the long term.

You have a great responsibility in this area, not only you will help protect the earth in long term, but also you can reduce cost in many areas. For hotel business, main sustainability pillars can be divided into three main areas which are Management & Efficiency, Planet and People.

Management and Efficiency

- Measure and reduce energy use.
- Measure and reduce water use.
- Identify and reduce waste.
- Identify and reduce carbon emissions.

Planet

- Reduce use of plastic products.
- Use of green, eco labeled cleaning products and chemicals.
- Serving of more vegetarian options.

People

- Community benefits

- Reduce inequalities

You can develop action plans for each of the above areas as a starting point to ensure your direct involvement in the world-wide sustainability efforts. Of course, some of the actions might require some initial investment which you should consider, when possible, especially the ones that will generate additional savings for you in the long run such as the use of solar energy.

The engineering department ensures the continuation of your business in efficient manner to ensure guest satisfaction and reduce cost.

A New Adventure

Pre-Opening

A New Adventure

Opening a new hotel is a pleasure and an amazing experience. It's possible that you are a member of the pre-opening team needed to start a new project. Whether it's your first time or not, every project is unique and has certain characteristics. Although hotels vary widely in terms of location, type, size, concept, etc., there are certain differences as well. Throughout my career, I had the opportunity to open a number of hotels—many, in fact, too many—so in this chapter I'd like to share some reflections and advice on this amazing journey.

Seeing a product come to life after several months of laborious effort has a unique quality that brings me immense joy and contentment. Managing a thriving hotel presents a unique set of emotions.

If you are a general manager, be prepared to be involved in a number of pre-opening activities and tasks that will keep you far busier than you may imagine. As you will be managing hundreds of issues and assigning hundreds of tasks to your teams, you must first establish a comprehensive filing system for yourself.

You do not want to become disoriented.

You are the project's main organizer and are in charge of organizing, coordinating, and following up to keep things going. You will most likely be working alone when you begin such a task, and you will be the first manager employed for the project. Yes, I realize that these are lonely times, but don't worry—this is your chance to demonstrate your abilities to both the owner and the management company. Soon, with all these trades, your role will become extremely important.

The extent of your involvement in the pre-opening process will vary based on your experience level and the part your management company plays. Since he handles numerous matters on behalf of the management company, the general manager must be hired approximately a year before the project opens.

Organization

First things first so settle into your workspace or office as soon as possible and begin building relationships with all the stakeholders involved. You will eventually need each of them.

As soon as this is determined, you must rapidly ascertain your immediate market area and its surroundings, including any suburbs, cities, resorts, or downtown areas. Go quickly and familiarize yourself. You'll be more productive in a short amount of time the sooner you establish this.

Orientation

The next stage is to familiarize yourself with the project as much as you can. You can accomplish this in a number of ways, but we advise you to begin with your own organization. They will be able to provide you with information about the project's specifics, its concept, and—most importantly—what its priorities are and its vision. At this point, copies of all project drawings, layouts, and other information will be provided to you.

You have, of course, already thoroughly read and considered your "Management Agreement" and "Technical Service Agreement."

It is imperative that you comprehend your company's vision and mission in addition to the legal relationship that binds the two parties.

Communication

You will slowly start to become the link between owner and company, and it is imperative that you speak the same language. The brief by owner and designer is of utmost importance and a critical step for you to understand the project details in full from both perspectives and what is to be accomplished.

"Make sure you seek to understand before being understood."

At this point, developing this habit is crucial. You will learn a great deal of information, so hold off on adding too much of your own thoughts and opinions now. You will have time to do so later. You will learn a lot in the first few weeks, and the idea will gradually become clearer.

You may want to offer some advice once you fully understand it and have gained the trust of your owners and other stakeholders, but only after talking with your management company.

Visibility

Develop the habit of being present at the project site; go there and take a tour every day, no matter what. You will serve as the business's eyes and ears in addition to the owner.

They'll look to you to provide regular updates on the situation from your perspective and will solicit your opinion on a variety of matters.

Pre-opening Budget

One of the top tasks you will be required to prepare early on is the pre-opening budget. Everyone will hunt you down to get this right.

The pre-opening budget includes several parts, consisting mainly of pre-opening labor costs for recruitment of staff, sales and marketing costs, collateral, technical service fees, a task force, training, and other miscellaneous expenses. In some cases, depending on the technical service agreement, they will include other material, such as opening supplies of amenities, collateral, and food products.

So as the captain of the ship, in order for you to prepare such a document, you have a lot of ground to cover in order to reach this stage.

Market Research

Probably, market research for the project has been completed prior to your arrival and is the basis for the decision to proceed with such a project.

You will further complete a detailed market research and competitive study to determine your competitive set, your potential market segments, and your feeder markets.

You will also need to complete a labor market study, including labor law requirements, to be able to establish your manning guide and benefit grid chart. Once this initial work has been completed, you will need to establish your countdown task list "month by month" until the opening date.

The projected opening date will be set by owners depending on project progress, but keep in mind that this will change several times depending on many factors that could delay the opening date.

You will eventually have to appoint a chief engineer as soon as possible, ideally 7-8 months before the opening date. It is imperative that he join the team early enough to fully understand the project's details. He will oversee the technical aspects of the project with contractors and serve as the main manager in charge of organizing future property maintenance and upkeep in order to protect the asset.

Mockup Room

When the mockup rooms—actual room samples made by the designer—are presented, your hotel's future appearance begins to take shape. This is how your hotel rooms or suites will appear in the future, and it will significantly affect how guests are welcomed.

You will be examining each and every detail of the mockup rooms with the assistance of your management company specialists in order to provide the owning company with feedback and come to an agreement on a final product that satisfies everyone. For the General Manager, this is a critical time.

You need to be completely involved in the process and engaged because soon you will need to receive all of the hotel rooms, which should have the same level of finish and product quality as the mockup rooms.

Operating Supplies

You will also be involved in many other details, such as the selection of operating supplies and other products. Make sure you refer to the consultants at all times during this stage.

"Coordinating between the different parties
is a key factor in your success."

To keep you involved, it's critical to monitor the situation and adhere to the project's timeframe. It is advised that you take a number of photos of the project status at several stage as it develops for documentation purposes, to write reports, and to share them frequently with your management company.

You are the project's eyes and ears, and as I mentioned before, you will make sure the predetermined vision stays on course.

Recruitment

A very important part of pre-opening tasks is the recruitment, hiring, and training of your teams. Usually, around six months prior to the opening date, you will recruit the Director of People Engagement to be on board, who will assist you with this huge task.

Depending on the pre-opening budget approved by the owner, your full team is preferred to be on board as early as three to four months before opening the hotel, but sometimes budget constraints do not allow it.

It is preferred to have your executive committee members on board five months out, department heads four months out, and the remainder of the assistants, supervisors, and ranking file about three months out. Each group of your team will have a set of detailed tasks to work on to set up their areas.

Sales and Marketing

The sales and marketing plan and activities that were laid out early on during the preparation of the pre-opening budget will be implemented in phases.

The timing of such activities must coincide with the correct opening date of the project to be effective. Your sales team will be in full motion during the last 90 days prior to the opening of the hotel to reach out to the agreed-upon market segments.

Project Delivery

The last ninety days prior to opening are very busy times and focused on receiving the hotel areas from the contractor, as well as all the necessary supplies, setup, and deep cleaning of all areas.

Along with these important tasks, your highest priority will be the induction and training of your employees to be ready and able to deliver the guest experience you seek. Your leadership skills, such as organization, planning, time management, and clear vision, are required during all these stages to coordinate the work and have a smooth and perfect opening.

You will lead and motivate the group to produce the high-caliber product and image that countless individuals have been slaving over for months to realize.

The time to deliver has arrived, and the hard work and dream will eventually come true.

License and Registration

One of the challenges in each project opening are the licenses required by the government in order to open the doors and run the business. Make sure you have understood well all the requirements for your country and work diligently with the help of your PRO "Government Relations Officer" or responsible person to obtain such licenses.

This process could be lengthy and require a lot of work and owner involvement to get it done.

Hotel Opening

It's opening day, and now is the right moment. To get to this point, you had to put in a lot of effort through many difficult moments and even frustrations. Yes, it's time for each member to give a performance. It's time to take a proud stance and greet your first visitor.

It's a wonderful feeling, so enjoy it and have fun. What happens next is a different story.

My Mind to Your Mind

Final Thoughts

My Mind to Your Mind

Now that you have reached this stage of the book and have understood well the leadership attributes and the operational priorities, what are you going to do with it? What are you going to change to be more successful? I can only imagine what you are thinking, but I want to share with you some thoughts that will help you on the road to success.

My Thoughts

- Love what you do.
- It all starts with you, so motivate yourself.
- You can do what you set your mind to do.
- Change is inevitable, and in many cases, it is great.
- Internal willingness and courage are needed.
- Take the first step and don't procrastinate.
- Be a better person and look deep into your ethics.
- Embrace knowledge and don't stop learning; it's never too late to start.
- Balance your personal and work lives.
- Don't worry, and be happy.

- Be understanding of people's needs and don't be selfish.

- Have the courage to fix what you broke.

- Block negative thoughts and practice power of positivity.

- Don't be lonely; there is always someone that you can talk to and bounce ideas off of.

- Solicit as much feedback as you can to know where you stand. Don't get surprised.

- Always seek win-win decisions for long-term gains.

- Present your work and yourself in a professional manner at all times.

- Encourage Millennials and use their ideas and energy to explore new ways.

- Build your team wisely and assess each person capabilities.

- Invest in the learning and development of your teams.

- Seek first to understand, then be understood.

- Everyone in the organization is part of your sales

- team; start with yourself.

- Guest engagement is our bread and butter, so stay connected at all times.

- Know your competition well.

- Ensure high levels of cleanliness and hygiene standards are met.

- Use different management styles depending on the situation to get best results.

- Embrace technology and use it to enhance productivity.

- Always maintain your product and don't fall behind.

- Be part of sustainability efforts to save our earth for future generations.

"Start now, and you can see the positive changes soon.

Just believe in yourself,

You can do it."